ARCTIC OCEAN

COLVILLE RIVER

NOATAK RIVER

KOBUK RIVER

KONUKUK RIVER

YUKON RIVER

FAIRBANKS

NORTON SOUND

YUKON RIVER

TANANA RIVER

MT. McKINLEY

SUSITNA RIVER

KUSKOKWIM RIVER

ANCHORAGE

KUSKOKWIM BAY

NUSHAGAK RIVER

HOMER

GULF OF ALASKA

JUNEAU

BRISTOL BAY

KODIAK ISLAND

PACIFIC OCEAN

Lake Clark National Park and Preserve

by Steve Kahn and Anne Coray

Photography by
Fred Hirschmann

Alaska Geographic Association
Anchorage, Alaska

Alaska Geographic Association thanks Lake Clark National Park and Preserve for their assistance in developing and reviewing this publication. Alaska Geographic works in partnership with the National Park Service to further public education and appreciation for national parks in Alaska. The publication of books, among other activities, supports and complements the National Park Service mission.

Authors: Steve Kahn and Anne Coray
Photography: Fred Hirschmann
Other Images: p.10, Robert Wheatley Collection, Anchorage Museum, B82.52.225; p. 14, © Field Museum #A107933; p. 20, photo courtesy of Helena Seversen Moses; p. 47, Huntington Library, San Marino, California, 39 (064); p. 50, Ward Wells, Ward Wells Collection, Anchorage Museum, B83.91.S0156.R17A; p. 52, photo courtesy of Helena Seversen Moses; p. 55, NPS Collections courtesy of Howard Bowman; p. 60, © 2009 William W. Bacon / AlaskaStock.com
Illustrations/Maps: Denise Ekstrand
Designer: Chris Byrd
Editor: Nora L. Deans
Project Coordinator: Lisa Oakley
National Park Service Coordinator: Mary McBurney
Song on page 12 was sung by Wass Trefon, recorded by John Coray, transcribed and edited by James Kari and is reproduced with permission from William W. Trefon, Sr., Craig Coray and James Kari.

Poem "Harvest" by Tom Sexton on page 35 reproduced with permission of the author.
Poem "Portage Creek Passage" by Mike Burwell on page 62 reproduced with permission of the author.

Alaska
Geographic

810 East Ninth Avenue
Anchorage, AK 99501
www.alaskageographic.org

Alaska Geographic is a nonprofit bookstore, publisher, educator, and supporter of Alaska's parks, forests, and refuges. Connecting people to Alaska's magnificent wildlands is at the core of our mission. A portion of every book sale directly supports educational and interpretive programs in Alaska's public lands. Learn more and become a supporting member at: **www.alaskageographic.org**

ISBN-13: 978-0-930931-84-1

Library of Congress Cataloging-in-Publication Data

Kahn, Steve.
  Lake Clark National Park and Preserve / by Steve Kahn and Anne Coray.
    p. cm.
  ISBN 978-0-930931-84-1 (softcover)
  1. Lake Clark National Park and Preserve (Alaska)--History. 2. Lake
Clark National Park and Preserve (Alaska)--Description and travel. 3.
Natural history--Alaska--Lake Clark National Park and Preserve. 4. Lake
Clark National Park and Preserve (Alaska)--Pictorial works. I. Coray,
Anne. II. Title.

  F912.C47K34 2009
  979.8'6--dc22
                    2008055543

Printed in China on recycled paper.

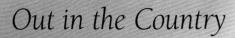

Out in the Country

LAKE CLARK NATIONAL PARK AND PRESERVE

CONTENTS

The Place of a Name

A tantalizing view of Redoubt and Iliamna Volcanoes presents itself on a clear day across the waters of Cook Inlet from the Kenai Peninsula. These towering volcanoes are just part of the rugged expanse of snow-covered peaks and nameless valleys of the Chigmit Mountains. Beyond the mountains are lakes, wild rivers, streams, and more mountains. And a body of water, Lake Clark, whose name serves as a touchstone for over 4 million acres of Alaska at its finest. As if it weren't enough, Lake Clark National Park and Preserve is so much more than land surrounding a spectacular mountain lake.

The Dena'ina Athabascan name for Lake Clark is *Qizhjeh Vena*, translating roughly, "many peoples gather lake." Today, most people know it as Lake Clark, after an expedition make in 1891 by John W. Clark of Nushagak and A.B. Schanz of the *Frank Leslie Illustrated Newspaper*. The Dena'ina know that this lake of rich resources that enticed people to gather at its shores is the nucleus, the starting point, from which grandness and diversity radiates out. It is a lake with great depth in a land with great appeal.

Lake Clark National Park and Preserve is the essence of the north contained in one national treasure. Within its borders are many of the biotic zones found in Alaska, including tundra, riparian, coastal, and forest. In alpine regions above Twin Lakes, extreme cold temperatures and brutal winds stunt much of the plant life, though numerous species of lichen flourish. At lower elevations, river and stream banks are lush with willows and grasses, while black and white spruce, birch, and poplar thrive in the boreal forests. In the coast's marine environment, a hybrid of white and Sitka spruce, known as the Lutz, ranges from just south of Tuxedni Bay to the park's southern boundary in Chinitna Bay.

Tremendous geologic forces have shaped the region. Massive glaciers once covered much of the land, forging deep U-shaped

valleys, carving saw-toothed ridges, and depositing piles of rubble called moraines. Glaciers, much smaller now, still cling to their rugged mountain homes, creating silt-laden waters that form streams, rivers, and numerous lakes.

This roadless wilderness provides habitat for numerous bird and animal populations. Wolverines and lynx roam over vast acreage. Dall porpoises, gray whales, and harbor seals swim in the dynamic waters of Cook Inlet. Brown bears feed on salmon and rake ripe blueberries into their waiting maws, and munch on coastal salt marsh vegetation.

A map of the area gives a visitor the first clues of what lies in wait. Points of interest are sometimes descriptive of color or shape, like Turquoise Lake or Double Glacier. They may contain a hint of abundant wildlife, with names like Moose Pasture Pass or Silver

Salmon Lakes. Goldpan Peak and Priest Rock suggest that humans have traveled through in search of riches or souls.

Much about the land is revealed in the Dena'ina practice of basing place names on important events or resources. *Valts'atnaq'* meaning *caribou hair stream* is the Dena'ina name for the upper Mulchatna River. *Nan Qelah Vetnu*, translating *moss is there stream*, is Miller Creek.

Regardless of the language, names are limited in their ability to fully encompass the scope and nuance of a region. The depth and breadth of a place like Lake Clark National Park and Preserve is not only inherent in its place names but also in the multitude of unnamed mountains, valleys, and streams, for which there is no better translation than sheer wonder.

Trails That Lead To and Away

What does it take to make a journey? A place to start from, something to leave behind. A road, a trail, or a river.

   —John Haines, *Living Off the Country*

Many park visitors are unaware of the rich, long history of the peoples of these lands, or who has lived in areas of the park and what first drew them here thousands of years ago. Like tiles in a great mosaic, clues help us form images of how prehistoric humans lived.

Exactly when humans arrived in Alaska is not known, but many anthropologists agree that the first people to colonize the landscape that is now Lake Clark National Park and Preserve arrived 14,000 years ago, sometime after the close of the Last Great Ice Age.

These nomadic people left few traces. We will never know what language they spoke or what their belief systems were, yet many aspects of their lives can be summarized from the remains of their camps. Archaeologists have learned that as early as 10,000 years ago hunters camped on knolls such as those in the northern part of the preserve, shaping and sharpening tools while watching for caribou. Wind-polished tools have been discovered in exposed, high altitude areas as evidence of prehistoric sheep hunters. From scant clues, scientists have learned that these people were not just big game hunters. They were resourceful foragers in coastal and interior environments, and fisherpeople as well.

Sometime after the Dena'ina speaking people settled in the Lake Clark area, their world was locked in a 500-year long cold snap from 1350 to 1900 A.D. Known as the Little Ice Age, it was characterized by widespread glacier advances, cold summers, and sudden shifts in climate.

It is estimated that Dena'ina Athabascans have occupied the region for at least a thousand years. The last several hundred years of their occupation is easier to piece together, largely from stories

Caribou Trails

A savvy hiker follows caribou trails when traversing alpine country; these conspicuous features provide firm footing for leather-booted bipeds. The trails are usually 14 to 18 inches wide, since caribou often travel single file when undisturbed. Watch carefully, though—the trails will weave, fork, and coalesce, so that one Alaskan Native has described them as resembling lines of wisdom etched into an elder's face.

handed down by Native elders. Prior to European contact, the Dena'ina led a semi-nomadic lifestyle, spending winters in *nichił*, partially underground log houses covered with a framework of spruce logs topped with birchbark. Their seasonal movements echoed patterns of the land: when the salmon arrived, the people set up fish camps; when game was abundant in an area, they took advantage of the opportunity to hunt or trap, usually traveling to do so. Dogs were primarily used as pack animals in these early times.

Not many generations ago, the Dena'ina made expeditions equipped almost entirely with materials provided by the natural world. From sinew and various kinds of wood they crafted sleds, snowshoes, backpacks, kayak frames, tools, and weapons. Their clothing included caribou hide shirts, leggings and boots, ground squirrel mittens and parkas, and gloves and caps from fur-bearing animals. Bear gut made an excellent waterproof shell, while salmon skin boots kept the feet dry. Grass formed a cushioning insole for all footgear.

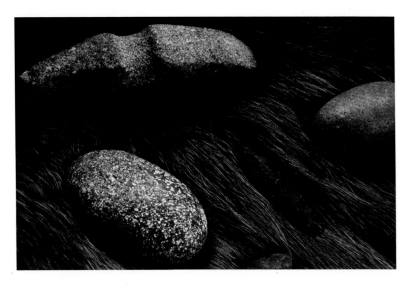

Artifacts found in Jay and Bella Hammond's garden near Priest Rock, not far from the Kijik Village site.

The people often put up temporary shelters. In the days before canvas and nylon, they fashioned a dome-shaped structure, or *skindulchin* from alder poles, using leafy boughs of the same tree for thatching. Grass or spruce bough flooring, a central hearth and smoke hole, and grass mattresses and caribou hides around the periphery completed the design. Another kind of "tent" was erected from brush. Birch bark sewn together with spruce roots served as a roof, which was packed into the mountains and left there for later use.

The Land Would Provide

Today, one of the routes historically traveled by the Dena'ina is in places indiscernible, overgrown with brush. The Telaquana Trail runs from the Old Village at the west end of Telaquana Lake south as far as *Qizhjeh Vena* (Lake Clark). Fifty miles long, the trail crosses stream valleys past Turquoise Lake and the headwaters of the Mulchatna and Chilikadrotna rivers, winds through low mountain passes, and traverses College Creek and the swift Kijik River. From there, the trail follows *Nan Qelah* (Miller Creek) and continues to Kijik Village.

In 2003, Frank Hill, a grandson of Mary Ann Trefon (who was part of the first Dena'ina family to settle permanently at Tanalian Point, near present-day Port Alsworth), reconnected with his ancestors by retracing the Telaquana Trail. With him were two brothers, a sister-in-law, and National Park Service historian John Branson.

Frank recalls that his grandmother Mary Ann and her family used the trail as a trade route for furs, flour, sugar, and tobacco. In *Sharing Our Pathways*, a newsletter of the Alaska Rural Systemic Initiation, he writes:

> *In contrast to our Dena'ina ancestors' simple and practical traveling and camping gear, we looked like we had supplies and equipment enough for a year-long safari!*

9

Dena'ina and Aleut peoples packed skin boats like these photographed in 1910 from Cook Inlet over the Iliamna Portage into the Bristol Bay watershed.

10

No doubt the ancestral Dena'ina possessed, more than modern man, an unwavering faith that the land would provide. Often it did, allowing them to supplement their dried salmon or moose with berries, trout, ptarmigan, or perhaps even a caribou, sheep, or bear they encountered along the way. When they stopped for the day near a freshwater stream, they would build a fire using grass, bark, and wood they had collected while walking.

Walking Dena'ina

The Dena'ina people traveled great distance by foot or boat for many reasons, often in search of food. Nevertheless, some excursions were motivated by more than the desire to fill the larder. Trade with other Native groups provided resources otherwise unavailable. Beads and iron fragments found at a Pedro Bay site and dating to the early 1700s suggest a pre-contact trade network with Siberia. From the coastal Dena'ina near present-day Tyonek and the Yup'ik residing on Bristol Bay, they procured clams, halibut, sea mammal pelts, and technology for building skin boats. The infiltration of trade goods into the Lake Clark region was augmented with the establishment of Russian posts, providing yet another reason for travel.

The Dena'ina covered a tremendous amount of territory, sometimes crossing glaciers, as they made forays through mountain corridors like Lake Clark and Merril passes. They followed the course of many rivers such as the Mulchatna and the Newhalen, while the Iliamna portage allowed them access to the marine environment of Cook Inlet. They trekked overland to reach drainages to the northwest as far as the Kuskokwim River. Given their willingness to travel such long distances, the inland Dena'ina have been referred to as the "Walking Dena'ina." Visits to other villages were frequent.

A testament to this long history of interaction is the earliest recording of Dena'ina songs and speech. Recorded in Nondalton in 1954 by John Coray, the songs incorporate many lan-

Goosetongue

You won't find goosetongue in most dictionaries, but you will find these wild greens on the Cook Inlet coast in salt marshes and along beaches. Best picked in the spring when the leaves are tender, goosetongue can be eaten raw or boiled, or can be frozen for later use. A delicacy, it is enjoyed by humans and bears alike. According to some Dena'ina, the use of goosetongue as food was passed on from the Russians.

11

guages: Dena'ina, Yup'ik, Slavic, English, and a rare dialect of Deg Xinag, formerly spoken on the upper Kuskokwim. Sometimes songs came by way of intertribal marriage, but they were also a trade item. Often considered commodities, they could be "purchased," or given as gifts.

The 1954 recording reveals that subjects for songs were virtually inexhaustible. There was a love song, a gambling song, a song about a man who was lost, another about a malamute pup. One man's composition was a candid account of the loneliness he experienced when his wife became ill and was flown to Anchorage:

> *Ts'iq'u yu niqu hne 'an yeha.*
>> Still for you I look there.
> *Nch'a eshchegh.*
>> I cry to you.
> *Nda ya t'ghesht'ih ni yahi yuk'hdi yihe?*
>> What can I do about it, in the sky there?
> *Nda ya t'ghesht'ih ni yahi yuk'hdi yihe?*
>> What can I do about it, in the sky there?
>
>> I look for you inside there.
>> I cry to you.
>> What can I do about it, in the sky there?
>> What can I do about it, in the sky there?
>
>> In an airplane I look for you there.
>> I cry to you.

> [spoken]
>> Look at this song that I made.
>> When you were staying there, staying in the hospital
>> I sang this.
>> Now do you see, do you understand?

In the days when airplanes were still a novelty, and "town" an abstract concept to indigenous peoples, Anchorage, located 160 air miles from Nondalton, must have seemed far away indeed.

Sophie Austin

Resourcefulness, coupled with an intimate knowledge of the land, provided Nondalton resident Sophie Austin a means of obtaining much-needed cash for her family. It was the 1940s. Using her dog team, Sophie ran a trapline, hauled freight, and cut cordwood for the school. She also delivered mail— once a month, for two years, she made the three-day run from Iliamna to Nondalton, Port Alsworth, and other places on Lake Clark.

Kijik village in 1902.

Qizhjeh Vena

The geometry is subtle. Moss-covered, raised squares or rectangles rest on the forest floor. The light has to be right, the grass not yet tall, to see beneath the canopy of spruce, birch, and cottonwood the faint tracings of a link to the past.

Located in broad lowland at the base of Kijik Mountain along the north shore of Lake Clark is one of the largest, most complex Athabascan archaeological resources known in Alaska. Charcoal samples, historic, and ethnographic evidence suggest a Dena'ina presence in the district 800 years ago, perhaps more. This archaeological treasure has yet to reveal all its secrets. Native elders and scientists alike believe the remains of many houses, cache pits, and artifacts are still to be discovered.

The site is of such significance in safeguarding information about the history and prehistory of the Dena'ina people that in 1995 it was designated a National Historic Landmark. Abundant resources, including timber, red salmon, large and small game, and plants and berries, continue to make the locale an integral part of the Dena'ina subsistence way of life, much as it was in decades past.

About 270 known prehistoric and historic house depressions lie in scattered clusters within the area. Also present are 2,500 to 3,000 underground fish cache pits, which may be the keystone of the extensive settlement's existence. Lined with spruce bark, these caches were used for fermentation and storage of sockeye salmon. It is believed that the people's ability to preserve such large volumes of protein-rich fish in such an innovative manner, in addition to more traditional methods of smoking and drying, permitted them a semi-sedentary lifestyle, one that could sustain a larger and more stable population than is typically found among other Athabascan groups. Fittingly, the Dena'ina name for Kijik Lake, *K'q'uya Vena* means "red salmon lake."

The best known and most recently occupied of at least 19 separate sites is *Qizhjeh Vena*, also known as Kijik Village. At the time of its first documentation by Russian explorer Peter Korsakovskii in 1818, Kijik had an estimated population of 150 people. About half of the homes were multi-room dwellings and housed more than one family.

The Kijik people were among the most isolated of the Dena'ina groups. Because they were not as accessible to early Russian and American influences, their population and traditional lifestyles were less disrupted than the Dena'ina ensconced on Cook Inlet and Iliamna Lake. In the late 1880s, however, a Russian Orthodox Church named St. Nicholas, crafted of hand-hewn logs joined with compound dovetail joints, was added to the complex at Kijik Village.

The village's cemetery swelled to several hundred graves due to a measles and influenza outbreak in 1902. With so many lost to these diseases, abandonment of the village ensued, culminating in 1909. The survivors moved 20-some miles southwest to establish a new home at Old Nondalton on Sixmile Lake. In subsequent years, the village was again relocated to a more favorable location. Today, Nondalton is a thriving community, whose residents, like those of the neighboring villages of Iliamna, Newhalen, and Pedro Bay, are still engaged in their Alaska Native subsistence and cultural heritage.

Surge and Sweep: Changing Landscapes

...when we don't live with birds or weather or waves we lose the opportunity to think hard about ourselves, to discover from nature important facts about human nature.

—Nancy Lord, *Fishcamp: Life on an Alaskan Shore*

As late as 2002, you could stand near East Glacier Creek at the mouth of Chinitna Bay and experience a time warp. Before you loomed a petrified tree, its trunk rising 50 feet or more from the smooth, sandy beach.

The top of the tree held fast to the surrounding sedimentary cliff; below the point of attachment was an aperture that resembled a Gothic arch. You stood in awe, mesmerized by one of nature's hewn cathedrals. It was easy to visualize wind and ocean waves tirelessly pummeling the siltstone at high tide, gradually widening the opening, incrementally exposing more of the petrified wood.

Maybe your imagination was transported further back in time: leaves grew on the tree—delicate, fan-shaped leaves, and you noticed the bark was rough and fissured, much like the bark of an aged cottonwood. Something stirred in your memory. You were in the presence of the oldest living tree species known to man: the *Ginkgo biloba*.

Surely you had set foot in China, the ginkgo's country of origin. But no—here you were on Alaska's Cook Inlet coast, on a tidewater beach , with a current climate incapable of supporting this exotic tropical tree.

Evidence of Change

Unlikely as it seems, there is evidence that ginkgo forests once inhabited parts of southern Alaska. Of course, this was millions of years ago, long before the Ice Age swept a frigid hand over much of the northern hemisphere. The petrified ginkgo on Chinitna Bay

collapsed finally in a winter storm, but photographs still serve as a reminder that geology is never stagnant: winds, tides, volcanic eruptions, rock slides, earthquakes, and glacial advances continue to shape and reshape the land, and accompanying climatic changes usher in new inhabitants.

Volcanoes

Geologic power lurks beneath the conical shapes of the park's Redoubt and Iliamna volcanoes. Active stratovolcanoes that rise over 10,000 feet, these grand glacial-clad peaks are composed of multiple layers of lava flows and pyroclastic rocks. Since historical observations began in 1778, Redoubt has erupted at least half a dozen times. The most recent—likely not the last—eruption in 2009 saw steam and ash blown to more than 12 miles above sea level. Although Iliamna has not erupted in recorded history, fumeroles on its east face frequently vent steam, an indication of continuing activity within the mountain. This mix of hot steam and gas indicates smoldering in the mountain's belly.

Flight

A pilot enters the rugged heart of Alaska in an open-cockpit airplane. The roar of the radial engine is muffled beneath his leather helmet. Protective goggles keep the wind from stinging his eyes, and his face smarts from exposure. The rigging of the biplane's wings hum a familiar tune.

A mosaic of gravel and sand bars fingered with swift-running channels stretches up the valley. Below him, the current sculpts the banks of the river. Willows and alder, birch and spruce, bend to the beat of the breeze. Above cascading waterfalls and talus slopes rise serrated ridges and rocky spires. The river narrows to a serpentine stretch of rapids, then widens again in boulder-strewn relief. The lure of side valleys, deeply scoured gullies, and alpine pastures turns the pilot's gaze left and right.

He travels above a land awash with variegated greens and grays, cutting the same air as hawks and bald eagles. Excitement sends a chill through his spine.

Or perhaps it is the brisk air, cooled by snow and hanging glaciers, that makes him shiver.

Pioneer aviator Russel Hyde Merrrill was one such adventurer. In early November of 1927, Merrill discovered a route through the Alaska Range. This low-elevation, 3,000-foot pass now bears his name. Located in the park's Neacola Mountains, it shortened the flying distance from Anchorage to the Kuskokwim region, saving pilots and passengers both time and money. One of the most scenic mountain passes in Alaska, Merrill Pass is also one of the most dangerous.

In 1930, a fellow pilot, Matt A. Nieminen, was possibly the first pilot to fly through Lake Clark Pass, another spectacular pass in the Aleutian Range. Lake Clark Pass would become one of the most frequently used airplane thoroughfares in the state.

Merrill's plane in front of Old Illiamna Village, July 1927.

In the midst of these processes, some life forms die out completely. Ammonites, for example, are not known after the Cretaceous period, which lasted 145 to 65 million years ago. All that is left of these spiral-shelled mollusks are fossilized remnants, formed when the organisms' decaying organic material was replaced with inorganic minerals found in groundwater, preserving these nautilus-like creatures in fossil form. Ammonite fossils, along with those of ancient bivalves, sea worms and plants, can be found at Fossil Point, near the park's northern coastal boundary. Amazingly intact, many of these fossils provide concrete examples of early life, giving clues to the area's prehistoric flora and fauna.

By contrast, trying to ascertain the genesis of colossal mountain formations such as the Alaska and Aleutian ranges is a continuous challenge. The Alaska Range extends for 400 miles from the Yukon boundary to its nexus with the Aleutian Range, an even longer 1,900-mile chain whose terminus is the Commander Islands, which straddle the International Date Line in the Pacific Ocean. Geologically speaking, these mountains are relatively new, and show as yet little erosion. Some peaks in the park's Chigmits and Neacolas thrust upward to heights of 7,000 and 8,000 feet, with the recently active Iliamna and Redoubt volcanoes measuring 10,016 and 10,197 feet, respectively. Visitors and residents alike may marvel, and wonder how these glaciated mountains came to be.

During the Jurassic period, around 180 million years ago, huge volumes of magma, or molten rock, worked their way upward. Finding escape routes through weak areas in the Earth's crust, great quantities of this magma ejected and formed mountains. Much of the magma failed to erupt, however, and instead cooled slowly and solidified into an underground batholith—a vast composite of diverse granitic rocks. Over the next 25 million years, other magma intruded

as the cooling batholith was squeezed upward. Thus, mountains in the Lake Clark and Iliamna region had their first beginnings.

Earthquakes and shifting tectonic plates further contributed to the building of the park's stunning massifs. Faults that lie in the valley system containing Lake Clark and the Tlikakila and Chokotonk rivers fractured and weakened the rocks. Wind, water, and ice chiseled and gouged, adding hollows and texture to the relief, a sculpting that, along with volcanic activity, continues today.

Most extraordinary was the ice. At least four major advances, known as the Brooks Lake Glaciation, occurred during the Pleistocene era (2 million to 10,000 years ago) in the Iliamna and Lake Clark region. Driven forward by the steady and unrelenting machinery we call glaciers, huge masses of ice filled older valleys and plowed into the landscape, and flowed southwest towards Iliamna Lake and Bristol Bay. It is impossible to imagine such power and immensity. Lake Clark itself is glacier-carved; the ice once stood roughly half a mile above the deepest part of the present-day lake, whose depth is estimated to be over 1,000 feet in some places. Many of the lakes on the northwest side of the park, such as Turquoise, Twin and Telaquana, sit behind glacial moraines, naturally formed dams made of rock debris sculpted by these Ice Age glaciers.

Needless to say, so much glacial ice doesn't melt overnight. In the 1940s the Tanaina Glacier spread across Lake Clark Pass; to clear it, a pilot had to fly 600 feet higher than he does today. Located near Summit Lake, this river of ice no longer spans the pass, but it remains one of the largest glaciers on the scenic route connecting central and southwestern Alaska. Its retreat continues at a steady rate. With the earth's current warming trend, there is every indication that Alaska's astonishing glaciers will diminish further in years to come, with a huge impact on the hydrology of the park.

Climate Change

Glacial melting provides dramatic evidence of climate change. More subtle to the untrained eye are changes in vegetation. On the Kenai Peninsula, recent studies indicate a shrinking of wetlands and an accompanying increase in the growth of shrubbery. As temperatures rise and bogs filled with sphagnum peat moss dry out, the ground is ready to support sturdier root systems. Regions that were once muskeg are being supplanted by blueberry bushes, dwarf birch, and black spruce.

Over time, it is possible that wetlands in coastal and interior areas of the park may be similarly affected. Some residents have observed alder encroachment on mountain slopes, an indication of climatic shift. Treeless valleys photographed in 1912 are now covered with the tenacious shrub. On Lake Clark, recent reports of robin sightings have been made into October and November, long after songbirds are known to depart for more temperate climes.

At various sites, ecologists have begun studying bark beetles as another means of assessing warming trends, since warm summers allow the insects to reach early maturation and enable the beetles to complete their life cycle in one year rather than two. These population outbreaks often kill acres of spruce forests. Thus far, minimal bark beetle presence is documented in the park's interior; however, the slow growth of these trees, as measured through core samples, indicates stress, and paves the way for future infestations. Beetle-killed trees have already been documented from Anchorage to Tuxedni Bay, and about two-thirds of Lake Clark Pass has been similarly affected.

Buffeted by Extremes

Generally speaking, the west side of the Cook Inlet coast experiences heavy snowfall in winter, while rain and fog is common during the summer months. This subpolar marine climate has annual precipitation levels roughly double that of the park's interior.

From Lake Clark to Telaquana Lake temperatures are colder than the coast's; Port Alsworth's record low in 1971 was minus 55° F; in 1969, Richard Proenneke recorded minus 51° F at Twin Lakes; in 1999, a two-and-a-half-week cold spell kept Lake Clark residents huddling around their wood stoves, while temperatures plummeted as low as the minus forties.

While such extreme cold may become increasingly rare, summers are typically warmer than those of the 1960s and 70s; Port Alsworth's 2004 high was 89°, topping the previous 86° record. From 2001 to 2005, Lake Clark did not freeze solidly three out of five winters.

Lake Fluctuation

The ocean may have tides, but lakes have seasonal fluctuations. Glacially fed lakes are particularly prone to variation. In summer, rapid snowmelt causes the water level to rise; as the temperature cools, melting ceases and precipitation falls in the mountains in the form of snow, which remains there until the process begins anew. Without the additional run-off, lake levels begin to descend. Lake Clark usually reaches its high water mark in July or August, and drops to its lowest point in the spring, averaging a 9-foot difference in depth. With the water at its ebb, formerly hidden rocks and reefs become exposed.

Nevertheless, Lake Clark has many predictable, though changeable, weather patterns. Sandwiched between high rugged mountains, the lake is often churned to a froth by gale-force east winds funneling through the pass, particularly in winter. These storms typically last two or three days. West wind generally brings moisture, and rarely builds to more than thirty knots. From the lower reaches of tundra near Telaquana, Twin, and Two lakes, bitter north winds find egress as they travel through College and Miller creeks.

Near Johnson River, on the coast, prevailing winds are from the north and south. Sometimes, a large southerly swell from a residual ocean storm may be counteracted by a northerly chop, creating confused seas that make navigation difficult. Tides also affect the coastal waters. Cook Inlet is known for its extreme tides, which can measure as high as 23 feet or as low as minus 5.

One of the most fascinating effects of weather is a mirage known as fata morgana, caused by a strong layering of cool air against water, sea ice, or land. Distant mountains, islands, or ships appear stretched upward, doubled, or inverted. Fata morgana can be observed in summer over the ocean and in winter over the land.

Steam Fog

There's nothing like fog to create atmosphere. A stillness descends—a hush. Deep water lakes like Lake Clark often produce steam fog in the late fall or winter, which forms when cool air moves over an open body of warmer water. Even in a cold year, the upper end of Lake Clark will not freeze over until late December. In recent years, as the Alaska climate continues to warm, this portion of the lake sometimes stays open all winter.

Sampling of Species

White spruce	*Picea glauca*
Black spruce	*Picea mariana*
Kenai birch	*Betula kenaica*
Balsam poplar	*Alnus incana*
Blueberry	*Vaccinium uliginosium*
Arctic grayling	*Thymallus arcticus*
Lake trout	*Salvelinus namaycush*
Northern pike	*Esox lucius*
Chinook/King salmon	*Oncorhynchus tshawytscha*
Coho/Silver salmon	*Oncorhynchus kisutch*
Sockeye/Red salmon	*Oncorhynchus nerka*
Mosquito	*Aedes communis*
Willow ptarmigan	*Lagopus lagopus*
Arctic loon	*Gavia arctica*
Bald eagle	*Haliaeetus leucocephalus*
Common raven	*Corvus corax*
Golden crowned sparrow	*Aonotrichia atricapilla*
American pipit	*Anthus rubescens*
Black-legged kittiwake	*Rissa tridactyla*
Harbor seal	*Phoca vitulina*
Wolf	*Canis lupus*
Lynx	*Lynx canadensis*
Wolverine	*Gulo gulo*
Black bear	*Ursus americanus*
Brown bear	*Ursus arctos*
Moose	*Alces alces*
Barren-ground caribou	*Rangifer tarandus arcticus*
Dall sheep	*Ovis dalli dalli*
Beaver	*Castor canadensis*

Spruce grouse feed on a variety of berries, flowers, and plants during the summer and fall. In winter spruce needles are the bird's sole source of nourishment.

Clockwise from top: white spruce, common loon, barren-ground caribou.

Sockeye Salmon

Sockeye salmon are commonly referred to as red salmon because of the vivid to dark red color on their sides and backs during the spawning season as well as the deep red of their flesh. Though they will spawn in streams and rivers, most populations are closely linked to lakes. In lake systems, the young salmon typically spend one or two years before heading to sea. Sockeye return to their home spawning area after residing in the ocean for one to four (usually two or three) years.

Both males and females die after spawning, but nutrients from the decomposing salmon carcasses fertilize zooplankton, a major food source for developing fry. Freshwater lakes, such as the park's Lake Clark and Kijik Lake, benefit immensely from the salmon's life cycle, the sharing of the ocean's bounty with relatively nutrient-poor inland systems. Phosphorous and nitrogen leaching from dead salmon fertilize streamside and lakeshore plants. A variety of animals, including bears, foxes, wolves, eagles, and ravens, not only feed on the spent bodies that wash up on shores and banks in late fall, they also transport nutrients to nearby terrestrial ecosystems as they carry salmon carcasses away from the water to feed.

Commercial, sport, and subsistence salmon fishing are intrinsic to the Bristol Bay area. Waters flow from the park and preserve into the Nushagak and Kvichak drainages, both habitat heavyweights in the world's largest wild sockeye runs. Studies suggest that trace amounts of copper in water may affect a salmon's olfactory sense and therefore interfere with its ability to locate its spawning grounds. Contaminants also threaten the health of the fish. For these reasons large scale development projects, including mining and oil and gas drilling, remain highly controversial in Bristol Bay and surrounding villages. Protecting the watershed necessary to maintain the sockeye salmon fishery in Bristol Bay and safeguarding habitat for fish and wildlife populations are fundamental management purposes of Lake Clark National Park and Preserve.

Q'ich'idya Was Last

I cannot expect to know the true names of animals, or how to call them to me, or the proper way to carry their tongues near my heart.

—Sherry Simpson, *The Way Winter Comes*

Something darts through the willows, revealing a flash of brown fur or slate gray feathers. On a sunlit ridge or in shadowed valleys beyond the summit are scurryings, boundings, explosions of wings. Much like the animals and birds that move across the land in ever-flowing fashion are the tales indigenous peoples share about the country that surrounds them. These stories, handed down from generation to generation, are sometimes offered in song.

To the east of Turquoise Lake a peak rises above eight thousand feet. This mountain is called Telaquana. A Dena'ina elder tells the story of a medicine man who struck his cane on top of the mountain, causing a crack to open in the rocks. The medicine man and *q'ich'idya* (pika), who was with him, looked inside to see all the animals on earth walking around. They both went into the mountain and *q'ich'idya* started to sing. He sang the names of all the animals. As each one heard its name, it emerged from the mountain: *gunsha* (ground squirrel), *vejex* (caribou), *yeghedishla* (black bear)… That is why, some believe, there are wild animals out in the country.

Q'ich'idya was the last to depart. Telequana closed up on the small creature, leaving half of him inside and the other half outside of the mountain. Maybe that is why a person only sees part of the pika peering out from behind the rocks in alpine regions.

Alpine Country

A shrill bark bounces from boulder to boulder—an early warning system echoing throughout the colony of hardy vegetarians. Perhaps a hawk, owl, or eagle is nearby. For ages the diminutive pika or "rock rabbit" has occupied old rock slides, talus slopes, and boulder-strewn country.

In the way that beavers collect deciduous trees, shrubs, and branches, pikas are the haymakers of high country, storing piles of clipped stems, twigs, and grasses for winter use. Beneath rock ledges, dried plants are stacked two to three feet high as evidence of the pika's summer of perpetual motion. Trails are worn into the hard earth by their tiny feet traveling countless times from nearby meadows and patches of vegetation.

Blueberries, azaleas, and mountain avens accent the pika's alpine home. From its burrow, the furry rodent may glimpse other, larger creatures—a band of caribou, perhaps, part of the Mulchatna herd, relaxing on a patch of snow or an exposed ridge, seeking the breezes of the high country to find freedom from the torment of

insects. Constantly moving, the herd travels in and out of the park, making appearances around Twin and Turquoise lakes and westward as far as Snipe Lake and the Bonanza Hills. Unlike moose, both male and female caribou grow antlers, though a mature bull is easy to distinguish because of its large size. By January, most bulls have dropped their antlers, while cows keep theirs until spring, the pregnant cows holding on to them the longest.

Sharing the alpine country is the Dall sheep, an impressive creature with honey-colored horns and a thick coat that allows it to endure harsh winter temperatures. This northernmost species of North American wild sheep numbers in the hundreds in the higher elevations of the park. The massive curling horns of mature rams arc gracefully around eyes possessing sterling vision—eyes that sweep the country below for danger, which most often materializes in the form of wolves, bears, or humans. Horns, which are not shed like antlers, produce annual growth rings that can be counted to determine an animal's age. Sixteen-year old rams and nineteen-year old ewes have been recorded, though twelve years of age is considered elderly for any sheep.

Studying the Wild

Various methods are used when studying wildlife population dynamics. Often park service scientists outfit large animals with radio collars to allow tracking of individual animals for the study of mortality rates, movements, and seasonal range use. Airplanes are also used to visually count animals. Moose surveys are best conducted in winter, when their brown bodies contrast with the snow. The optimum time to count sheep is prior to snowfall, because they are concentrated in large nursery groups and their white coats are easy to distinguish from the landscape.

The Lake Clark area does not have an abundance of moose, as compared to other parts of the state, but the park population has remained stable enough to allow local residents a subsistence hunt for bulls. The movement of moose into the park and preserve is relatively recent—in the 1930s few sightings were reported. No one knows for sure why their presence was scarce in years past. Factors that influence moose populations include lack of food supply, creation of new forage areas by wildfires, changes in hunting pressure, climate change, and predation.

Currants

Though blueberries and raspberries make excellent jams, the beautiful but tart red currant is a favorite berry for jelly enthusiasts. Watch for the translucent clusters in late summer or early fall.

> *…I tumble down the bank of my own dream*
> *to our secret place*
> *where I reach out for those globed fruit*
> *each one holding its drop of light*
> *waiting for you to make it jell.*
>
> —Tom Sexton, *Harvest*

Moose

In the lower elevations, an herbivore is busy munching on the park's abundant willows—the majestic moose. It may wander down even farther as summer wears on, seeking out ponds or marshes that yield bountiful quantities of grasses, sedges, or water lily roots. Moose can keep their heads under water for incredible lengths of time while feeding; when a head is raised, strings of vegetation may still be hanging from the animal's mouth or antlers, giving the enormous ungulate a comical and pseudo-amphibious look.

The interconnectedness of the myriad species of flora and fauna is a mystery of giant proportions. What triggers a summer infestation of aphids or an autumn explosion of mourning cloak butterflies is often unknown. When studying population surges, scientists may benefit from the knowledge of long-time local residents, who contribute their observations of plant and animal shifts: one year, porcupines are plentiful; the next, coyotes appear and the porcupines all but vanish, after which wolves move into the country to displace the coyotes. A keen eye may notice that a field normally erupting with wild geranium will produce mostly lupine the following year. Proliferation of black currants in one area does not guarantee that these berries will be available for the next harvest.

It may appear, on the surface, that plant growth is most affected by temperature and precipitation levels, while bird and animal populations are primarily influenced by predation and food supply. Here is where the equation becomes complicated. When trying to work through the maze of population impacts, one encounters numerous detours and side trails that often intertangle but seldom reveal a single conclusive answer to increases or declines in a given species.

Seabirds and Swans

Chisik and Duck islands, just off the coast of the park in Cook Inlet, are breeding colonies for more than 30,000 seabirds, including horned puffins, black-legged kittiwakes, common murres, pigeon guillemots, and black oystercatchers. This may seem like a large number; however, the count is roughly half of what it was in 2001. With minimal threat from foxes, weasels, and mink, the islands' rocky cliffs have traditionally served as island fortresses, the sheer quantity of birds providing a stronghold against most predators. Today that defense is weakening, as bald eagles and ravens increase their attacks

Clam-digging Bears

Serious clam-diggers need the right technique, maybe one they learned from their mother or from watching other bears. They might sit on their haunches to do their excavating, or stand on all fours and rake the sand, thrusting their snouts down to capture their meals. Bears' dining habits vary too, ranging from a careless crunch and gulp (shells and all) to the more refined practice of prying the shell apart with two or three claws. The most efficient bears can uncover up to 100 clams during a low tide.

on vulnerable chicks. One explanation is a decrease in herring and salmon, which have until recently been a mainstay for eagles.

Besides predation, starvation is a major player in the seabirds decline on these islands. Although the puffins' diet includes seaweed and algae, they, like other alcids, rely heavily on energy-rich fish such as sand lance and capelin. Unfortunately, nearshore waters that have historically attracted copious runs of these important protein sources are warming, causing fish to seek cooler temperatures in deeper parts of the ocean. Birds that are not deep-water divers, like kittiwakes, experience increased difficulty in procuring food. Others, such as murres, must travel greater distances to find sustenance for their chicks.

An island domicile is no guarantee of a specie's survival, but it certainly has advantages. No wonder castles in the Middle Ages were surrounded by moats. Building its own "island" nest in undisturbed marshy areas of the park is the world's largest member of the waterfowl family, the trumpeter swan. A trumpeter builds a mound for its nest from 6 to 12 feet in diameter that sits one to two feet above the surface of the water—not a shabby method of discouraging invaders.

The trumpeter's recovery story is a happy one. In 1932, biologists knew of only 69 trumpeters in the wild in the Continental United States. After the termination of market hunting for skins and meat, the population rebounded enough to be taken off the endangered species list. Alaska wildlands, like the protected ponds, lakes, and marshes of Lake Clark National Park, have long been a sanctuary for thousands of trumpeters and even greater numbers of tundra swans. Trumpeters are very sensitive to human disturbance, especially near their nesting sites. These majestic birds need protected habitat to continue to thrive—room to spread their wings, as it were.

Alpine Tundra Nesting Shorebirds

If chickadees, redpolls, and nuthatches are remarkable for the fact that they over-winter in Alaska, equally astounding are the migrations of alpine tundra nesting shorebirds. After spending summers in the far north, surfbirds (above), wandering tattlers, Baird's sandpipers, and American golden plovers sometimes set their internal compasses for South America. The little Baird's, whose length is but seven inches, may fly all the way to Tierra del Fuego. This sandpiper is known to cover a distance of 4,000 miles nonstop.

The Turquoise Lake area of the park has recently been named a globally Important Bird Area (IBA) by the National Audubon Society because of its rare and unique assemblage of alpine tundra nesting shorebirds. Found in high plateaus between Twin and Telaquana lakes, shorebirds are attracted to gravel bars and disturbed landscapes, especially the arid, lichen-covered ground of recessional glacial moraines.

Brown Bears

Bears are opportunistic omnivores. Living both high and low, they feast according to what's available, consuming sedges, grasses, roots, fish, insects, berries, mammals, carrion and—if humans are careless, garbage. Diverse habitats of Lake Clark National Park and Preserve offer a variety of food. A bruin found in the park's marine-influenced environs along Cook Inlet may munch on several species of mollusks, including the tasty razor clam, though it would seldom dine on ground squirrels. For a bear inhabiting the mountains near Twin Lakes, the inverse would be true.

Bears residing in interior regions are commonly called grizzlies, their coastal counterparts, brown bears. After extensive study based largely on skull similarities, scientists agree that the brown bear and the grizzly are the same species, *Ursus arctos*. The hair color of both runs the spectrum of brown, from blonde to nearly black, though males tend to be darker than the females.

Grizzlies don't grow as large as coastal bears, and have a lower population density, probably due to a less plentiful food supply. Salmon contribute to the summer protein intake for most bears, but the amount varies widely depending on the proximity to easy fishing. Inland bears have to work harder for their meals, traveling greater distances at higher elevations for less caloric intake. Some people claim that the grizzlies in inland Alaska are less tolerant of humans and are more apt to run away, or in rare instances, to charge.

Brown bears have an obvious shoulder hump, which is one of several characteristics that separates them from their cousin and fellow park resident, the black bear. Though some grow larger, most brown/grizzly adult males weigh from 500-900 pounds. The female is generally 25 to 50 percent smaller. Bears have been recorded to gain almost two pounds a day during peak feeding seasons, resulting in fat stored on the rump in excess of six inches deep. By contrast, they lose about 20 percent of their weight during the winter spent in the den.

Despite their bulk, bears are amazingly fast, using their powerful muscles to move adeptly across all kinds of terrain, from rocky ridge to salt marsh. A keen sense of smell allows them to detect odors many miles distant. It is no surprise that this awesome and sometimes intimidating behemoth of the animal kingdom is at the top of the food chain.

Histrionicus *histrionicus*

Rushing clear water streams often surrounded by forest provide breeding habitat for one of our prettiest northern sea ducks. The male harlequin is particularly striking, its white spots and stripes and chestnut-hued flanks accentuating a slate blue body. Not surprisingly, the duck's Latin name, Histrionicus, derives from histrio, or stage player. The male's markings are said to resemble the tights worn by pantomime buffoons.

The female, in typical duck fashion, is more modest, sporting but two or three white spots on the side of her dusky brown head. She is easily confused with her look-alike, the female bufflehead.

Known as a "torrent" duck, the harlequin, like the American dipper, walks on the bottom of swift streams when foraging. In summer, the harlequin depends primarily on aquatic insects for nourishment, especially the larvae of midges, blackflies, caddisflies, and stoneflies, which thrive in highly oxygenated mountain streams; in winter, its diet is replete with intertidal delectables such as crabs, limpets, periwinkles, and mussels. It may also snatch an occasional fish.

Harlequins nest throughout the park, from Telaquana and Turquoise lakes in the interior, to streams such as West Glacier Creek and Spring Creek along the Cook Inlet coastline. The female usually lays six to eight eggs, and the male promptly departs as she begins her 28 to 30 day incubation. Ducklings, with no power of flight, have been seen bobbing joyfully in waterfalls and rapids—surely the equivalent of child's play.

Because of the duck's fondness for exposed shorelines, coastal harlequins are often seen perched on rocks. Harlequins make great subjects for photographers. Sometimes males will pair up, their spectacular plumage an easy eye-catcher for even a novice birder.

The Many Colors of Gold

From Alaska's mountains, woods, and waters, I've gleaned an
abundant fortune in coin of the spirit, if not of the realm.

—Jay Hammond, *Tales of Alaska's Bush Rat Govenor*

In the spring of 1778, the aptly named ships, *Resolution* and *Discovery* carried Captain James Cook and crew through the murky waters and strong tides of the inlet now bearing his name. At the time, Cook Inlet was sparsely populated, with just a smattering of Native villages. The first European to make official contact with the coastal Dena'ina, Cook also made initial notation of Redoubt Volcano, which would become part of Lake Clark National Park and Preserve.

Other British and Spanish explorers followed closely in Cook's wake. When the *Discovery* returned again in 1794, it was piloted by Captain George Vancouver, who sailed up the inlet's west side. Impressed by the "lofty, rugged mountains" that included Iliamna Volcano, Vancouver anchored his ship in Tuxedni and Chinitna bays. Leaving his assistant, Peter Puget, to investigate these uncharted waters, he continued northeast and noted an established Russian fort near Tyonek. This post, along with one at Iliamna Lake, was among 40 Russia would build during its occupation of Alaska, which lasted until the United States purchased the territory in 1867.

Russia's interest in Alaska was piqued in 1742, after survivors of the tragic Bering expedition returned to Kamchatka with more than tales of hardship and endurance. On their backs and rolled into bundles were pelts of blue fox, fur seal, and sea otter—the latter in particular of immense value, such that it triggered a surge of exploration and exploitation by the fearless *promyshlenniki*, free-lance exploiters of natural resources. China, with whom Russia had finally reached a trade agreement after years of haggling, set the price. One sea otter skin could earn a Russian clerk an entire year's income!

Before long, Russia had laid claim to Alaska. With no government, the new colony had free rein, and it wasn't until the formation of the Russian American Company in 1799 that some conservation measures were put into effect. One goal its founder, Nicolai Rezanov, laid down was to "control all exploitative activity from hunting to mining." Rezanov made certain this directive was enforced after visiting the Pribilof Islands a few years later, where he witnessed the sickening and wasteful slaughter of fur seals. In 20 years, the herd had been cut down by 90 percent.

The sea otter was also in decline. By the late 1810s pelts were rare, prompting the Russians to send in an expedition to assess the fur and mineral potential of the Interior, including the Lake Clark and Iliamna Lake region. Thanks to another conservation policy implemented by Governor Ferdinand von Wrangell, both fur seals and sea otters showed recovery by 1850.

Father Vasili Shishkin, center, flanked by two deacons, photographed at Nushagak about 1885. By the 1830s Russian Orthodox priests traveled regularly in the Illiamna/Lake Clark region performing baptisms and conducting services. Father Shishkin visited Kijik Village in 1878. Cape Shishkin, on the northwest shore of Lake Clark, still bears his name. The Orthodox faith remains widely practiced in southwest Alaska.

Alas, with the purchase of Alaska by the United States, Russia's conservation measures were abandoned. By 1890 in some areas, including Chinitna Bay, once "the richest sea otter hunting ground in the Kadiak district," according to a U.S. Government report, the 80-pound white-whiskered "Old Man of the Sea" was all but exterminated. No longer commercially viable, the sea otter was given protection under the 1911 Fur Seal Treaty. Although a brief harvest was reinstated in 1967, the sea otter currently enjoys sanctuary from all but Alaska Native hunters under the federal government's Marine Mammal Protection Act.

The inland Dena'ina did not deal directly in the sea otter industry, yet they were heavily impacted by it. Russian influence came in the form of clothing, cookware, iron tools, and an occasional firearm. Despite early hostilities between the cultures, the Dena'ina Athabascans eventually adopted the Russian Orthodox faith. People intermarried, so that names like Nicolai, Alexie, Evanoff, Rickteroff, and Karshekoff became common.

When *odinochkas*, Russian trading posts, were established on Iliamna Lake and on the Nushagak and Kuskokwim rivers, the Dena'ina spent more time trapping, using their catch to barter for commercial items like flour, salt meat, butter, and cloth, as well as sugar, tea, and rum. Not long after the United States' acquisition of Alaska, the center for trade shifted to A.C. Point on Cook Inlet, where the Alaska Commercial Company set up operations.

With the growth of the Bristol Bay fishery, the construction of new trading posts on Iliamna Lake, and the influx of white settlers and schools, the Dena'ina became increasingly accustomed to a cash economy. They did not, however, relinquish their subsistence lifestyle. Today, the people still depend on the land's bountiful resources for both sustenance and supplemental income. The importance of salmon as a mainstay for residents throughout the park cannot be overemphasized.

Nudelvegh

Sockeye salmon spawn in Lake Clark from late August through mid-September. This doesn't mean the fishing season is over, however. Native elders still enjoy eating salmon that is netted sometimes into late October, then hung on racks to dry. Called nudelvegh, *this form of dried fish has a mild flavor, and the concept of utilizing a resource after it has been given the chance to reproduce has obvious ecological advantages.*

Gillnetting the Hard Way

Double-ender sailboats were introduced in the late 1800s for commercial salmon fishing in Bristol Bay. Most of the vessels were just under thirty feet long, and constructed of cedar or fir planks and oak frames. The two-person crew used oars when the wind was calm. Over eight thousand of these boats were made for the Alaska market. The sturdy boats, essentially a beefed-up design of Columbia River boats with extra ribbing, could hold as many as three thousand salmon. In 1950 a federal regulation preventing the use of motorized vessels was repealed and sailboats soon dropped out of use in Bristol Bay.

One of the few restored double-enders in existence sits on permanent diplay at Lake Clark National Park and Preserve's Visitor Center in Port Alsworth. The boat, number 23 in its fleet, was brought north to Lake Clark in the 1950s by John Coray. In the late 1990s the boat was donated to the park by the Al Ward family.

The Growth of the Bristol Bay Fishery

The watershed that feeds Bristol Bay provides for some of the greatest numbers of spawning sockeye salmon in the world. Before returning to their home waters, the quintessential sockeye, or "red" salmon typically spend two or three years in ocean waters feeding on zooplankton, larvae, small fish, and squid. Lake-associated water systems are the target for most populations as they travel up rivers to spawn in stream outlets and inlets and along rocky shores.

Salmon are bound to the Lake Clark region socially, environmentally, and economically. Congress acknowledged their importance, setting down, as one purpose of the park's establishment, to "protect the watershed necessary for the perpetuation of the red salmon fishery in Bristol Bay."

Commercial fishing began in Bristol Bay in the early 1880s. Euro-Americans and Asians were brought in to fish and work the canneries, whose numbers increased to at least a dozen by the turn of the century. Though local Dena'ina were seldom employed in the early years of the industry, they felt its effect when overfishing depleted the number of salmon available for subsistence purposes. Their eventual involvement as cannery workers and fishermen constituted a major introduction to wage employment and the English language.

The fishery found its way through years of growing pains. Normal annual fluctuations in the number of returning salmon were exacerbated by intensive fishing and the use of fish traps and barricades. Years of good runs, high demand, or high prices were followed by disaster. The so-called "conservation measure" of banning power boats in the early 1920s, that lead to an almost thirty-year reign of sailboats in Bristol Bay, was likely more of an attempt by unions to control the fishermen than to protect the fish.

Alaska statehood in 1959 saw salmon traps outlawed and an increase in the number of independent fishermen plying the waters of the bay. (Traps had already been banned in the Nushagak area.)

Further efforts were introduced to both stabilize the industry and protect the resource. Two of the most notable restrictions were the "limited entry permit" and the establishment of a 200-mile limit on foreign fishermen. Economic problems and weaker runs in recent years have caused concern over the industry's future. Sound management and protection of the habitat upon which salmon populations depend are the keys to keeping the fishery and the salmon as resources for perpetuity.

Settling the Region

Spurred in part by the fishing industry, Europeans gradually moved into the Lake Clark country. Shortly after the turn of the twentieth century, a young Norwegian laid down permanent roots near Portage Creek on Lake Clark. Brynild Clover, or Brown Carlson, as he came to be called, was of short stature but powerful build. Before journeying inland, Carlson worked as a commercial fisherman in Bristol Bay, and on sailing ships as a youth. He had circumnavigated the globe, yet he often claimed, "This is the best place in the world. Right here, on Brown's beach." He backed up his boast by living on his property for nearly sixty years.

The difficulties of making a living in the remote wilderness proved no obstacle for Carlson. He dabbled in prospecting, recording the first gold claim on the lake in 1911 and working periodically for Fred Bowman, who began operating a placer mine on Portage Creek in the late 1930s. Brown's capital, however, was in the furs he trapped.

Taking five days to run, his 100-mile long trapline began at his cabin and extended into Lake Clark Pass, continued to Otter and Lachbuna Lakes, then followed the Kijik River Valley back to Lake Clark. Carlson traveled on foot, using pack dogs to help transport supplies. His catch included red fox, lynx, land otter, beaver, wolverine, and marten, along with an occasional mink or wolf.

Mary Ann **Kitulkilgih** *Trefon*

Mary Ann Trefon was born around 1880 and raised in a village on the Mulchatna River. She and her husband, Trefon Balluta, first settled at Telaquana Village in the late 1890s. Then they moved to Kijik, Old Iliamna, and Tanalian Point in pursuit of economic, religious, and educational opportunities. Trefon died in the mid-1920s. Mary Ann raised their youngest children at Tanalian Point and later moved to Nondalton. Among her descendants are village chiefs, musicians, song leaders, and respected elders. The story of this strong and resourceful woman unfolds as a continuing tribute to family ties and Dena'ina lifeways.

Like Carlson, others who settled in and around the park were dependent upon the land. Often these hardy souls trapped and fished, including coastal residents George Brown and Joe Munger. Also on the Cook Inlet coast, Wilber Morris, utilizing the area's abundant white spruce, established a commercial sawmill operation near Red Glacier. In 1919, the Surf Packing Company started a salmon and clam canning operation at Snug Harbor on Chisik Island, which is now part of the Alaska Maritime National Wildlife Refuge.

Tanalian Point

White prospectors were the first non-Alaska Natives to reside at Tanalian Point, located on the south shore of 45-mile long Lake Clark. A 1925 Bureau of Fisheries report suggests the area was inhabited since 1895. Among the early residents was J.W. Walker, who filed a 160-acre homestead claim in 1912. The land was never patented. By 1920, ten people were living at Tanalian Point, including Walker's friends Joe Kackley and Otis M. "Doc" Dutton, along with Trefon Balluta and Mary Ann Trefon's family. In addition to mining and trapping, Kackley and Dutton assumed the occasional role of schoolteacher, teaching Alec, Pete, and Katie Trefon to read and write.

Charlie Denison, another intrepid sourdough, moved to Lake Clark in 1932, settling near Tanalian Point several years later. A sawmill operator and green-thumb gardener, Denison later wedded a mail-order bride, Frieda Reidi, of Switzerland.

With the advent of dependable aircraft suitable for bush travel, land that included protected waters gained increasing appeal. In 1944, Mary and Leon "Babe" Alsworth staked a homestead at Tanalian Point, a decision precipitated by the property's location on sheltered Hardenburg Bay. The bay, almost circular in shape, is blocked from harsh winds by surrounding spruce forests and Osprey Island. On the south side of the island a narrow channel affords a landing and take-off "strip" for float planes. Alsworth also cleared a runway for wheeled aircraft, which was extended to 3,000 feet by 1950.

Tanalian Point was renamed Port Alsworth, and is currently home to approximately 100 year-round residents, including employees of Lake Clark National Park and Preserve. Port Alsworth is also a base of operations for numerous fishing lodges. Clients seeking trophy fish are typically flown to outlying "hot spots" located south and west of Lake Clark.

Mining

Prospecting attracted many people to the Lake Clark area in the late 19th and early 20th centuries. In 1906, Charles Brooks and Charles von Hardenburg staked mining claims on Kasna Creek, a small stream flowing into Kontrashibuna Lake. Copper and iron were the primary minerals of interest.

One of the greatest challenges to the Kasna Creek project and the Bowman Gold mine was the importation of heavy equipment.

Fred Bowman (right) and his son, Howard (left) at Portage Creek. The Bowmans began mining Portage Creek for gold in 1939, working portions of nine claims

The only feasible route ran fifteen-and-a-half miles from Williamsport on Cook Inlet to Iliamna Lake. A former bear trail, the Iliamna Portage was traversed in the early days with pack horses or dog teams. From Iliamna, another sixteen miles up the Newhalen River led one to Nondalton, where boats could be hired for the trip up Lake Clark. Finally, there was the daunting task of cutting trails through unspoiled forest in order to reach the mining claims.

Joe Thompson, who lived in the area for decades, took a more modest approach to mining. For several summers in the 1960s, Thompson made the same two-hour hike up the mountain behind his cabin. There, on a rocky ridge, he chipped single-handedly at the stubborn ground, hoping to unearth a pocket of ore large enough to transform his dreams into tangible assets. It was not to be. He left Lake Clark an old man, the most visible evidence of his stay a humble, 12 by 17-foot cabin roofed with gas can "shingles," and a rusty shovel lying at the bottom of a 6-foot hole on the slope of what the Dena'ina call "Ghost People's Mountain." Whatever the reasons—lack of revenue, an unwillingness to assume the debt of a large loan, perhaps—Thompson's footprint upon the land was slight.

"Locking it Open"

On December 2, 1980, Lake Clark National Park and Preserve was established under President Jimmy Carter and the Alaska National Interest Lands Conservation Act (ANILCA). As with national parks across the nation, protection and maintenance of the area's resources and wilderness was the incentive behind the park's creation.

Rather than prohibiting hunting, fishing, and other activities, ANILCA made allowances for "customary and traditional use" of resources by local residents. Though disputes occasionally arise about "who gets what," it is important to remember that sacrifice of some privilege is often necessary to insure sustainability. The degree to which we are willing to accept our roles and responsibilities in the

Wild Rivers

Three of Lake Clark National Park and Preserve's rivers are designated as National Wild Rivers, which protects the waters and associated environments as areas for public use and enjoyment. The Tlikakila, Mulchatna, and Chilikadrotna were chosen for their natural qualities, including primitive shorelines with little sign of human presence, and exceptional recreational, scenic, fish, and wildlife values.

The entire length of the swift, glacially influenced Tlikakila lies within the park's boundaries, where spectacular views of the Neacola and Chigmit mountains' rugged summits, glaciers, and waterfalls await float trip enthusiasts. Turquoise Lake gives birth to the Mulchatna, which begins as a shallow waterway, then gains volume and turns to whitewater as it passes the history-rich mining area of Bonanza Hills. Long stretches of exciting yet navigable rapids make "the Chili," as locals call the Chilikadrotna, which flows out of Twin Lakes, one of the best river runs in the region.

care and management of this incredible natural heritage, and the intelligence and respect we bring to our discussions of regulations and procedures, will play a crucial role in the park's future.

Surely those who have flown over this expanse of jutting, mountainous terrain, who have been mesmerized by ridge after ridge ablaze with fireweed in August, who have spent a few quiet days in the backcountry observing the antics of a weasel or watching a red fox pounce on voles, view such protection less as a prudent course of action than as an imperative.

The most common access to the park and preserve is by air charter. A one to two-hour flight via small aircraft equipped with wheels, skis, or floats can be made from cities along the road system, such as Anchorage, Kenai, and Homer. Touching down in Port Alsworth, on a mountain lake, or at select places on the coast, travelers can be left alone to hike, kayak, raft, canoe, or simply camp out.

With no roads, developed campgrounds or established trails in the park (other than the two-and-a-half mile trail to Tanalian Falls near Port Alsworth), hikers and campers must be well prepared and self-sufficient. Weather delays often occur. Prior to setting out on a wilderness adventure, careful map screening and terrain and climate consultation with park service personnel at the field headquarters and Visitors Center in Port Alsworth, or the field office in Homer, is advised. Park staff can also point out where within the park and preserve some lands are privately owned and should be respected, usually near lakes or coastal shorelines.

Although visitors may come any time of year, most arrive between June and September, often seeking guided wilderness adventures from commercial operators specializing in fishing, bear viewing, or sightseeing in the spectacular habitats of Lake Clark National Park and Preserve.

Richard Proenneke

Simple living is a catch phrase familiar to many but practiced by few. One of those rare individuals to pursue this principle was Richard Proenneke, who spent thirty years on Twin Lakes, in what appears to have been utter contentment. Driven by nagging questions about self-sufficiency and his ability to withstand isolation from his fellow man, Proenneke, at 51, set out to prove that he could rely almost entirely on his own wits and physical stamina.

His first requirement was a cabin. For its construction, he elected to use only hand tools: a double-bitted ax for felling trees, a rip saw to make lumber, and augers, chisels, and gouges for fine-tuning his craftsmanship. Whenever possible, his materials were provided by the land. His roof was covered with sod. He fashioned wooden hinges for his door. He even built his own furniture.

Proenneke's diet was modest. In all his years at Twin Lakes, he took only one sheep. He ate numerous fish and cultivated a small garden. His supplemental food and supplies were flown in by bush pilot Babe Alsworth, often Proenneke's only human contact throughout many long, cold winters. This is not to say that he was without companions. The gray jays in particular were fond of him, frequently perching on his shoulder for handouts like blueberry hotcakes or sourdough biscuits.

Hardly a man to seek fame, his journals, edited by Sam Keith under the title *One Man's Wilderness*, published in 1973, nevertheless earned him an international reputation. The book was translated into Japanese, and a documentary based on the text has been featured on television in the United States. Lake Clark park historian John Branson is annotating his complete journals into a trio of publications documenting all thirty years of Proenneke's solitary life deep within the park.

Jay Hammond

In his book, *Tales of Alaska's Bush Rat Governor*, Jay Hammond expressed relief when his second term expired in 1982, and he and his wife, Bella, were able to return to their Lake Clark homestead at Miller Creek. Juneau had been taxing, and he was happy to be home, free of external obligations.

Nonetheless, it wasn't long before he agreed to narrate a television program, titled "Jay Hammond's Alaska," which, in broadcaster Larry Holstrom's words, would be "an upbeat celebration of those colorful folk who've found their lives and longings better fulfilled in Alaska than anywhere else." The program was one of many commitments Hammond would make in the ensuing years, commitments that inevitably pulled him away from his wilderness abode.

Arguably, no other Alaskan has taken the role of public servant so seriously. He served on the board of the National Audubon Society. He gave graduation addresses. He spoke to the Nature Conservancy, the World Bank, and the Pioneer's Home. In fact, he was in such high demand that one year he was asked to do 13 speaking engagements in a single month. Until 2001, at least one leg of these trips—getting to Anchorage—was often made in his own Cessna, which he piloted.

Though the former governor liked to refer to himself as a "reluctant politician," making presentations to an engaged audience had obvious appeal for him. He was a natural-born speaker, with a gift for metaphor and a self-deprecating wit. People loved his easily recognizable, gravelly voice. They often referred to him as "Governor Jay."

Despite his attraction to the limelight, Hammond had a reflective side, and a deep appreciation for wild places. He referred to Alaska's "crown jewels," his phrase for areas protected under the Alaska National Interest Lands Conservation Act and offered, in support of this legislation, a classic Hammond inversion: "Rather than being 'locked up' as some contend, these jewels are being locked open, for the enjoyment of all."

Rivers, mountains, lakes, and clean air drew him back, time and again, to his Miller Creek cabin, with its splendid view of the Currant Creek Valley and the Chigmit Mountains. It is fitting that he ended his life there, surrounded by family. This revered Alaskan, who possessed such charm and humility, was buried August 3rd, 2005, on his property, at a site he chose himself.

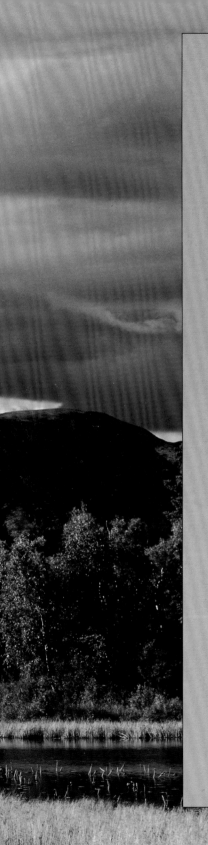

Portage Creek Passage

by Mike Burwell

For my friends this is summer history: the hike
to the ridge for lake vista and blueberries.
We move up canyon slowly through bugs, brush,
falling homesteads; ford creeks, claw up slopes
to this broad ridge above their cabin.
For hours we stoop to berries, are drawn
to the gold of saxifrage, arnica,
the violet of monkshood and geranium.

We come to a prospect hole.
At the bottom, a rusting shovel, artifact
of dream, failure, their silences
still lodged in this high earth. Before them,
Native feet and song, some laughter
passed up canyon to this place of portage
and down the divide to a distant stream
running toward the headwaters of the Mulchatna.

Above we find clouds and sun; below,
the turquoise lake water. We climb
to a higher ridge where we see
on a brushy divide a brown bear sow
and her three cubs. She is a pulsing chocolate
heart, the cubs small brown exhalations
exploding from her for berries, inhalations
running back to exchange their joy.

As this caravan of fur expands, contracts,
flows over the brushy flat,
we take in the strength of this wild event,
their movement through to feed
passing lightly, silently,
without bending anything more corporeal

than our luck today to touch their passage.